AMAZING
SNAKES
AND REPTILES

AMAZING
SNAKES
AND REPTILES

Sandy Creek
NEW YORK

An Imprint of Sterling Publishing
387 Park Avenue South
New York, NY 10016

Editorial and design by
Amber Books Ltd
74–77 White Lion Street
London N1 9PF
United Kingdom

Contributing Authors: David Alderton, Susan Barraclough, Per Christiansen, Kieron Connolly,
Paula Hammond, Tom Jackson, Claudia Martin, Carl Mehling, Veronica Ross, Sarah Uttridge
Consulting Editor: Per Christiansen
Series Editor: Sarah Uttridge
Editorial Assistant: Kieron Connolly
Designer: Andrew Easton
Picture Research: Terry Forshaw

ISBN 978-1-4351-4278-7

For information about custom editions, special sales, and premium and corporate purchases, please contact
Sterling Special Sales at 800-805-5489 or specialsales@sterlingpublishing.com.

Manufactured in China

Lot #:
2 4 6 8 10 9 7 5 3 1
09/12

Contents

Introduction

The class of reptiles includes a range of creatures such as snakes, lizards, turtles, crocodiles, iguanas, geckos, and many more. They have been around since the age of dinosaurs and can be found today all around the world. They are cold-blooded and have armored or scaly skin. They can be tiny or huge, ferocious, or timid.

American Copperhead

The American copperhead will try to find a place where it can lie in wait for a mouse or a vole that it can ambush. But it also hunts and seeks out caterpillars. A young copperhead uses its brightly colored tail to attract a frog (that thinks the tail is a worm). It then eats the frog.

WHERE DO THEY LIVE?

In northern Mexico and the southern and eastern USA, from Texas to Massachusetts.

USA

Mexico

Camouflage

▶ If a human passes, the snake will freeze and, hidden in a heap of dead leaves, will be almost invisible.

Venomous

◀ These snakes are venomous, but they are generally not aggressive. They will only usually bite if stepped on. The bites are painful to humans but not usually fatal.

FACTS

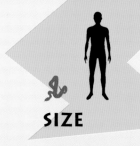

SIZE

• Adults usually grow to 20–37 in (50–95 cm).

• They have heat-sensitive pits below their eyes to find prey.

• Their venom destroys their prey's blood.

DID YOU KNOW?

A young copperhead looks like an adult but is lighter in color and has a yellow tip on its tail.

Bites to humans can cause intense pain, tingling, throbbing, swelling, and nausea, and can also damage muscles and nerves.

When disturbed, a copperhead can produce a smell like cucumbers.

Behavior

▶ In the southern United States, in the hot summer months, the copperhead is active at night. During the spring and fall, when it is cooler, it is active during the day. From October to February it returns to dens to hibernate. These dens may contain many snakes and will be used year after year.

Anaconda

The anaconda is the most powerful of the giant snakes. It uses its massive coils to squeeze the life out of prey that seems too large to eat. The green anaconda is the largest snake in the world. It can be up to 24 ft 9 in (7.6 m) long. It stalks prey in the swamps and rivers of tropical South America. It feeds on fish or caimans and even jaguars and small deer.

Huge Middle

▶ The anaconda is huge but it is the massive circumference of its middle, at nearly 3 ft (1 m), that is most remarkable.

DID YOU KNOW?

It can take weeks for an anaconda to digest one meal. It can live for months between meals.

It can stay underwater for as long as 10 minutes before it needs to come up for air.

Its huge jaws are attached by stretchy ligaments that allow it to swallow its prey whole.

WHERE DO THEY LIVE?

The tropical rain forests of South America and the swamp areas of Trinidad.

Trinidad

South America

Hunting

▶ An anaconda will hunt on land, but it prefers to stay in the water, where its huge body feels less bulky. To hunt, it lies at the surface of a stream or pond waiting for an animal to stop by for a drink or a rest. Its nostrils are on the top of its snout, so it can breathe while it is almost entirely under the water. Its teeth point backward, to help draw prey deeper into the snake's mouth.

Oval Eyes

◀ The anaconda has no eyelids but its eyes are protected by a layer of skin called the brille. The oval-shaped pupil at the center of the eye helps it to see by night.

FACTS

SIZE

● Moving on land, it leaves behind a deep, wide trench.

● The average size is 20 ft (6.1 m).

● The female green anaconda is larger than the male.

Asian Cobra

The Asian cobra is longer than men are tall. It has a deadly bite that paralyzes muscles and can cause heart attacks in humans, killing them. Some cobras can squirt venom directly into their victim's eyes. It lives in plains, jungles, fields, and near human populations.

Hooded Neck

▶ The Asian cobra spreads out its hooded neck to make itself look even bigger and scarier.

WHERE DO THEY LIVE?

All over southern and southeastern Asia, from India to southern China and the Philippines.

Asia

Feeding

◀ They eat other snakes, lizards, and other reptiles. They will also eat frogs, birds and birds' eggs, large insects, and small mammals such as mongooses.

FACTS

● It grows up to 6 ft (2 m) long.

● Symptoms from bites appear from 15 minutes to two hours later.

● It lives from sea level up to 6,600 ft (2,000 m).

SIZE

DID YOU KNOW?

🖐 This snake is respected and feared in Hindu culture. The god Shiva is often shown with a cobra at his side.

🖐 It is often seen with snake charmers. In fact, the cobra is deaf to the snake charmer's music, but it feels the foot vibrations and follows with its eyes the guide given by the charmer.

Snake Pattern

▶ The Asian cobra is sometimes called the spectacled cobra because of the pattern of two circles linked together on the back of its head. The spectacle pattern on the snake varies from snake to snake. Also, the color varies, but it is usually yellowish, black, or dark brown, with lighter markings on the throat.

Basilisk Lizard

As long as the basilisk lizard weighs less than 7 oz (200 g), it can escape a predator by running on water. It does this by slapping down hard on the water, creating a "hole" of air. The water pressure around this air pushes the foot up again. But with each step it sinks a little deeper and finally has to swim.

Breathing

▶ Basilisk lizards are excellent swimmers and they can stay underwater for up to 30 minutes.

DID YOU KNOW?

🐾 The lizard's tail acts as a counterweight, helping it balance and stay upright when it is running.

🐾 Even when asleep, the basilisk holds on to bushes or trees.

🐾 For a person to sprint on water, they would need to run at 62 mph (100 km/h) and have the leg strength of 15 people.

WHERE DO THEY LIVE?

From southern Mexico south through Central America to Ecuador, Colombia, and Venezuela.

Central America

South America

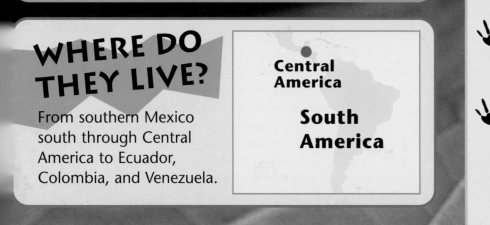

Lizard Diet

▶ Part of the iguana family, basilisk lizards are omnivores. This means that they eat both animal and plant matter. They eat worms, scorpions, and shrimp, as well as lizards, small birds, fish, and mice. They will also feed on fruit and flowers. The male (pictured here) has a crest on the back of its its head. It is also sometimes known as the double-crested basilisk.

Feet

◀ The hind feet have a tiny fringe of skin running around the five toes. This increases the foot's surface area when hitting the water, but collapses when pulled out, helping it move.

FACTS

SIZE

● Males are larger than females and grow up to 3 ft (1 m).

● Some males weigh up to 20 oz (600 g).

● They live for more than seven years.

Bearded Dragon

This Australian lizard puffs out its throat pouch to reveal a "beard" of sharp-looking spines. It does this to scare off rivals or attackers. In fact, the spines are actually fairly soft and harmless. The bearded dragon bobs its head to show who's boss and waves its hands to show respect.

Fireflies

▶ Bearded dragons cannot eat fireflies and other animals that produce light. This is because the light chemicals are poisonous.

WHERE DO THEY LIVE?

Australia

The seven species of bearded dragon are found all across Australia.

Good Eyesight

◀ It relies mainly on its excellent eyesight to find prey. Enlarged scales around the eyes help to keep out sand and dirt blowing in the semidesert landscape.

FACTS

SIZE

- They grow to around 18–24 in (45–60 cm) long.
- One-third of its total length is its tail.
- They live for five to six years.

DID YOU KNOW?

🖐 The legs of a bearded dragon are small but it can run extremely fast to escape from predators.

🖐 Some species of bearded dragon are kept as pets because they are friendly and relatively calm.

🖐 Males and females are about the same size, although males usually have a larger head.

Feeding Time

▶ As omnivores, they eat both meat and plant matter. They mainly eat crickets, as well as leafy greens such as parsley and celery. They also eat fly larvae, locusts, silkworms, and flower greens, such as dandelion greens and rose petals. In captivity they will also eat non-citrus fruits such as strawberries.

Black Mamba

The black mamba is the largest venomous snake in Africa. It is also the fastest snake in the world. It has been recorded moving at 10–12 mph (16–19 km/h) over a short distance. It has no natural predators except man, and will attack if it has no other choices.

Eyes

▶ The glassy, lidless eyes have round pupils that shrink to limit the light they let in. Snakes with round pupils hunt by day.

WHERE DO THEY LIVE?

Africa

In grassy savannahs, clearings, scrub, and open woodlands in eastern and southern Africa.

Home

◀ It is a territorial snake with a favorite home. This is usually an abandoned termite mound, a hollow tree, or a rock crevice. It will defend its territory.

FACTS

SIZE

● It grows up to 14 ft (4.3 m) long.

● It has no external ears but can sense vibrations.

● The black mamba's venom is the fastest-acting of any snake.

DID YOU KNOW?

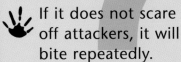 When threatened, it raises a third of its body off the ground and hisses. When it attacks, it makes several quick strikes, and then escapes as quickly as it can.

If it does not scare off attackers, it will bite repeatedly.

It generally stays away from humans, but its bite can kill people.

Dark Mouth

▶ Its jawbones are loosely connected so that it can stretch them apart to swallow victims that are much bigger than its own head. It is called a black mamba because the inside of its mouth is dark blue to inky black. It shows this coloring when it is threatened, and spreads its neck-flap like a cobra. It eats rats, mice, squirrels, bats, and small chickens.

Boa Constrictor

The boa constrictor eats capybara, mice, rats, lizards, and small birds. It kills by grabbing its prey in its jaws and coiling its body around the victim. Then, each time the boa breathes out, it tightens its grip, until it suffocates the animal. The boa's ribs stretch to make room for the animal it has eaten.

Swimming

▶ Not only can it move quickly on land, but the boa can also swim well. It often lives beside rivers, lakes, or marshes.

WHERE DO THEY LIVE?

They are found from dry scrub to rain forests in Central and South America.

Central America

South America

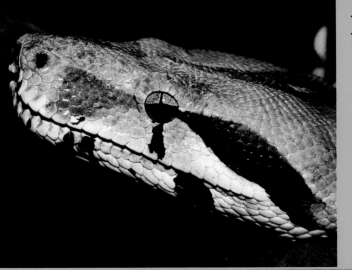

Head

◀ The eyes are small but they have vertical pupils. These open wide at night to let in as much light as possible. The tongue collects scent molecules from the air.

FACTS

SIZE

- They are usually between 6 ft 6 in and 12 ft 6 in (2–4m).
- They can weigh up to 33 lb (15 kg).
- They can live up to 40 years in captivity.

DID YOU KNOW?

🖑 Most snakes usually have one lung, but the boa constrictor has two.

🖑 It has ridges like claws on its body. These were once hind legs from when the boa developed from being a lizard.

🖑 In areas with cold or dry spells, the boa can stay still in a burrow for weeks without feeding.

Camouflage

▶ The boa is camouflaged from predators and prey. In rain forests, it has bold, bright markings that hide it in the tropical background. In sandy, open areas it has much paler markings. The boa can sense heat from cells on its mouth. Females are usually longer and wider than males.

Boomslang

By day, the boomslang hangs very still in trees and bushes, waiting for victims. It is looking for chameleons, frogs, birds, and small mammals. When it sees a target, it catches the prey between its jaws. The boomslang injects venom that makes the victim bleed from all the holes in its body. Then the boomslang swallows its prey headfirst.

DID YOU KNOW?

- The boomslang would prefer to scare a human away than attack it.

- The word "boomslang" means "tree snake" in the South African language Afrikaans.

- A female leaves her eggs in hollow tree trunks or in rotting logs.

Mouth

▶ It has a very wide mouth. Its deadly venom runs down its three fangs into the body of its victim.

WHERE DO THEY LIVE?

In habitats from scrub to savannahs in sub-Saharan Africa.

Sahara Desert

Africa

Large Eyes

◀ Its eyes are very large and its pupils are round. It has excellent eyesight and will move its head side to side to get a better view of what is in front.

FACTS

SIZE

● It can grow up to 6 ft (2 m) long.

● Hatchlings up to 1 ft 5 in (45 cm) long are harmless to humans.

● Its venom can kill humans.

Boomslang Body

▶ Adults come in many colors. Females are usually olive green or brown, but males can be mixtures of black, green, red, yellow, and even blue. Young boomslang are all the same: they have brown heads, white chins, and bodies with brown or gray speckles. The scales are arranged in diagonal stripes. They have a ridge down the center. Their head are shaped like eggs.

Bush Viper

There are nine species of bush vipers. Most of the species live in trees. They eat small amphibians, lizards, rodents, birds, and even other snakes. Usually they ambush prey from hanging positions on tree branches. They keep hold of the prey until the venom has killed the prey. Then they swallow the prey.

WHERE DO THEY LIVE?

Africa

They live in grasslands, mountain regions, and forests in the part of Africa on the equator.

Tongue

▶ Like most snakes, the tongue can pick up scents from the air. That way it can find its prey.

Ambush

◀ The bush viper has a prehensile tail, which means the tail can grip. It coils its tail around a low tree branch, hangs its head down, and waits for an unsuspecting victim to pass by.

FACTS

SIZE

• It grows up to 29 in (75 cm) long.

• Its venom causes bleeding in humans.

• Vipers have the longest fangs of all snakes.

DID YOU KNOW?

🖐 The venom is stored in the head, in the glands that hold saliva.

🖐 The ridges on the scales help it grip to tree branches. Those of the hairy bush viper stick out like spiky bristles.

🖐 Some bush vipers have pale tips to their tails. They are thought to wiggle them like maggots to attract prey.

Different Species

▶ This is a horned bush viper (*Atheris ceratophora*), but all bush viper species have a wide, triangular head. The eyes are quite large with oval pupils. The scales overlap and have ridges. The species have many different colors, from green and brown to yellow and black. These snakes use color and skin patterns as camouflage.

Bushmaster

Unlike most pit vipers, the female bushmaster does not give birth to live young; she lays eggs. These she guards fiercely against rats and other snakes. It takes the eggs two months to hatch. The female stays coiled around them for much of this time. A bushmaster can still hunt if its eyes are covered, but it can't hunt properly if the heat-sensitive pits behind its nostrils are blocked.

WHERE DO THEY LIVE?

Central America

South America

They are found in lowland rain forests in Central and South America.

Pit Organs

▶ The pit organ sensors in its head allow it to find prey through the heat the prey produce. This way it can hunt in the dark.

Jawbones

◀ Like most snakes, the bushmaster can dislocate its jawbones to stretch its mouth around the bodies of its victims. Then it swallows them whole.

FACTS

SIZE

- Adults range from 7 ft 6 in to 11 ft 6 in (2.4–3.5 m) long.

- On average, 12 eggs are laid in each clutch.

- It can survive on fewer than 10 large meals a year.

DID YOU KNOW?

✋ At night, the vertical pupils of the eyes open wide to catch as much light as possible.

✋ Newborn bushmaster hatchlings are more colorful than adults.

✋ Even the bite of a young bushmaster can kill, but bushmasters do not often have contact with humans.

Warning Signs

▶ It thrashes at plants with its tail to warn off enemies. It makes a sound a bit like a rattlesnake with the scales on its tail. If this doesn't scare off an attacker, it will bite and may release its venom. Some small prey it can eat alive without using its venom. It eats small mammals, birds, and reptiles.

Chuckwalla

The chuckwalla is harmless to humans. Its reaction to threat is to run away. It then hides itself in a tight rock crevice. There it inflates its lungs in order to wedge itself in the crevice. Neither birds of prey nor coyotes will be able to reach it—or if they can, they won't be able to extract it from its hiding place. It is active during the day.

Tail

▶ It thrashes its tail when trying to escape. In prehistoric times it had sharp spines along its tail.

WHERE DO THEY LIVE?

They are found in arid (dry) areas in California and Mexico.

USA

Mexico

Laying Eggs

◀ Females breed only in years when there has been enough rainfall. Five to 16 eggs are laid between June and August. The eggs will then hatch in September.

FACTS

- It is up to 24 in (60 cm) long.

- It weighs up to 4–5 lb (2 kg).

- It can live for up to 25 years.

SIZE

DID YOU KNOW?

🖐 They are mainly herbivorous, eating leaves and fruit.

🖐 When freshwater is not available, an island species of chuckwalla in the bay of California drinks saltwater instead.

🖐 The word "chuckwalla" comes from the Native American Cahuilla Shoshone tribes of southeastern California.

Plump Body

▶ Around the neck and shoulders the skin is loose and wrinkly. When the lungs inflate, the skin unfolds to enable the body to expand. The main body is quite plump, which means it can store food for a long period of time in the desert. The body is also flat, so that it can slide into rock holes. The scales on the body help give grip in crevices of rocks.

Cottonmouth

The cottonmouth is a venomous snake from the pit viper group. It gets its name from the white inside of its mouth, which it displays when threatened. It is the world's only semiaquatic viper: it is usually found in or near water such as slow-moving streams, shallow lakes, and marshes. It is a strong swimmer and will swim into the sea.

WHERE DO THEY LIVE?

They are found in waterways in the southeast USA on the Atlantic Coast and the Gulf of Mexico.

USA ●

Gulf of Mexico

DID YOU KNOW?

Even when it is dead, it can react and bite if picked up.

On some islands in the Gulf of Mexico, cottonmouths gather beneath the nests of seabirds to feed on small newborns that fall out.

Bites on humans hurt and cause long-term damage, but do not kill.

Diet and Predators

▶ Cottonmouths mainly eat fish and frogs. They are preyed upon by snapping turtles, American alligators, horned owls, eagles, red-shouldered hawks, herons, cranes, and egrets. They are also sometimes eaten by other cottonmouths. Baby cottonmouths have bright yellow tips to their tails. These might be to attract prey. Then the cottonmouths will attack.

Day and Night

▶ It hunts in water at night, but it isn't shy of being seen during the day. It can be seen warming itself in the sun.

Under Threat

◀ When the cottonmouth feels threatened, it throws its head back and opens its mouth wide. It shakes its tail and makes a loud hiss.

FACTS

● They are up to 6 ft 3 in (1.9 m) long.

● The head has heat sensors that help it to find prey at night.

● Newborns are 8.75 in–1 ft 1 in (22–35 cm).

SIZE

Death Adder

The death adder lies very still on the ground among dry leaves. The only thing moving is the end of its tail, which it waggles. A mouse sees the tail waggling and mistakes it for a worm. The mouse approaches the adder and quickly the adder's jaws seize the mouse and gobble it up.

Speed

▶ When the death adder attacks, it is the fastest-moving snake in the world.

WHERE DO THEY LIVE?

They are found across Australia and in southern New Guinea.

New Guinea

Australia

Wedged Head

◄ The death adder has a head shaped like a wedge. This holds a massive venom gland. When its fangs wear out, they are swallowed. New fangs replace the old ones.

FACTS

SIZE

- They grow up to 3 ft (1 m) long.

- The fangs are 0.25 in (6 mm) long.

- They are among the most venomous snakes in the world.

DID YOU KNOW?

🖐 They eat rodents, lizards, frogs, and small birds.

🖐 Death adders were originally thought to be vipers because of their triangular heads and short, strong bodies.

🖐 The non-venomous New Guinea boa is known to mimic the death adder to scare off predators.

Deadly Venom

▶ The death adder's small fangs cannot bite very deeply into a person's skin. However, even a shallow bite is enough. Sometimes symptoms don't appear for up to 48 hours, but in one bite it can inject more than three times the venom needed to kill a human. Its venom paralyzes the body, stopping it from breathing and so killing it.

Desert Horned Viper

If the desert horned viper feels threatened, it rubs its scales together to make a loud, rasping sound. This is to frighten away any predators. If this doesn't work, the viper can strike very quickly. When angry, it swishes its tail like a cat.

WHERE DO THEY LIVE?

They are found across North Africa and the Middle East.

Middle East

Africa

Fangs

▶ Before attacking, the fangs come out of their protective sheaths. They pierce the skin of their prey, injecting venom.

Head

◀ The female is larger than the male, but the male has a bigger head and bigger eyes. Although it's called a horned viper, it doesn't always have horns.

FACTS

SIZE

- It is 24–29 in (60–75 cm) long.
- In captivity it can live for up to 17 years.
- A female lays between eight and 23 eggs.

DID YOU KNOW?

It avoids the extreme desert temperatures by burying itself, then it waits for suitable prey to pass by.

North African snake charmers often use desert horned vipers in their acts.

Its venom is not very toxic for humans, but does cause swelling, bleeding, and vomiting.

Sidewinding Snake

▶ They like dry, sandy areas with rocky outcroppings. They move by sidewinding. To do this, they press their weight into the sand or soil and move sideways. They move this way because they are on soft or slippery surfaces like sand, rather than on hard edges. They usually hunt at night when the temperature drops and other animals are out hunting.

European Adder

If a European adder finds a nest of mice or birds, it may eat the whole family. When two male adders fight over a female adder, they stick up their heads, wrap their bodies around each other, and try to push each other over. This is called the "dance of the adders" and can last 30 minutes.

Sunshine

▶ When a European adder lies in the sun, it flattens its body as much as possible to expose its skin to the sun's heat.

WHERE DO THEY LIVE?

They are found across northern Europe (except Ireland), and across Asia to northern China.

Europe

Asia

Camouflage

◀ The adder has a dark zigzag pattern down its back. This hides it from enemies such as birds of prey by making the outline of the snake's body irregular.

FACTS

SIZE

- Adults can grow to 35 in (90 cm) in length.

- These snakes weigh between 2 and 6 oz (50–180 g).

- European adders hibernate in winter.

DID YOU KNOW?

🖐 The European adder and the common grass snake are the only snake species found inside the Arctic Circle.

🖐 The European adder is not aggressive and will only bite when stepped on or picked up.

🖐 If there is a hint of danger, it will usually disappear into the undergrowth.

Snake Senses

▶ Its eyes have vertical slits for pupils in the center. This is usual in snakes that hunt at night, which the European adder does in the warmer parts of its range. Its strongest sense is its tongue. From this it can "taste" the air for prey. The male is usually gray and black; the female is brown.

Flying Lizard

When the flying lizard runs into trouble, it simply leaps into the air, spreads its "wings," and glides to safety on the bark of another rain forest tree. Its wings may not look like a bird's, but they allow the flying lizard to land where it wants. It can live in trees except for when the female lays eggs in the soil.

Gliding

▶ They can cover up to 197 ft (60 m) in a single glide. They can move between forest trees without touching the ground.

WHERE DO THEY LIVE?

Asia

In southeast Asia in the rain forests of Malaysia, Indonesia, and the Philippines.

Wings

◀ It doesn't have real wings, which would be attached to its arms. Instead, its "wings" are flaps of skin attached to its movable ribs.

FACTS

SIZE

• They are about 8 in (20 cm) long.

• They cannot fly; they can only glide.

• They are also known as "butterfly lizards."

DID YOU KNOW?

🐾 As it glides through the air, the flying lizard steers itself by lashing its long, slender tail from side to side.

🐾 It is territorial, with a male marking two or three trees as its own. A few females will live in each tree.

🐾 The flying lizard never glides when it is raining or windy.

Dewlap

▶ It has a short, sticky tongue to eat insects. It eats ants found in trees, and termites. Beneath its chin it also has a flap of skin that can extend. This is called a dewlap. On males, dewlaps can be bright yellow; on females they can be sky blue. A male will usually extend his "wings" and his dewlap if he meets a new flying lizard or feels threatened.

Frilled Lizard

There are many predators for the frilled lizard on the ground. It can be attacked by snakes, wildcats, and birds of prey. Its first defense is to be very still and hope not to be noticed. If that fails, it raises its huge frill and hisses repeatedly. If this fails too, it runs away.

WHERE DO THEY LIVE?

New Guinea

Australia

They are found in northern Australia and southern New Guinea.

Mouth

▶ To add to the effect of its frill, it opens its mouth and shows its teeth and the pink inside of its mouth.

Defense

◀ The frilled lizard is all about putting on a show. It can rear up on its hind legs and lash the air with its claws, jaws, and tail to try to scare off predators.

FACTS

SIZE

- It can weigh up to 1 lb 8 oz (700 g).
- In the wild it lives for about five years.
- The frill is 8–12 in (20–30 cm) wide.

DID YOU KNOW?

🖐 The frilled female lizard sometimes hops like a kangaroo, especially when cornered, to try to scare off a predator.

🖐 It spends most of its time in trees, eating insects and smaller lizards.

🖐 At first it only lived in Australia, but millions of years ago it expanded its range to New Guinea.

The Frill

▶ The frill is a U-shaped flap of skin, open at the back of the neck and supported on each side by two bony rods. The male has a bigger and brighter frill than the female. Apart from defense, it raises its frill to scare off other males and to impress females. The frill might also help warm the lizard in the sun and cool it down in a breeze.

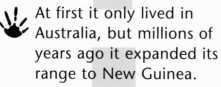

Gila Monster

The Gila monster's body is covered with bony, bead-like scales. Its bite can be very painful and is full of venom, which can kill reptiles, rodents, or rabbits. Male Gila monsters bite each other, but are immune to the venom. Strangely, the venom has little effect on frogs.

Tough Armor

▶ Its scales do not overlap. They make a tough armor and help hold in moisture in the desert heat.

WHERE DO THEY LIVE?

They are found in the southwestern USA and northwestern Mexico.

USA

Mexico

Habitat

◀ They live in woodland, scrubland, and deserts that have some vegetation. They can climb trees and cacti in search of eggs.

FACTS

SIZE

- They grow 16–22 in (40–55 cm) long.

- They live for about 20 years in the wild.

- They weigh 10–12 lb (4–5 kg).

DID YOU KNOW?

✋ It takes its name from the Gila River in southwest Arizona, USA.

✋ It has been known to live for three years without eating. In this time it survives off fat reserves in its tail.

✋ So many Gila monsters have been kept as exotic pets that they are now rare and protected by law.

Eating and Hunting

▶ It is a heavy, slow-moving lizard and feeds on bird and reptile eggs, small birds, mammals, frogs, lizards, insects, and animals it finds that are already dead. It only eats five to ten times a year, but it might eat up to one-third of its weight when it does. It uses its strong sense of smell to find prey, even sniffing out and digging up buried eggs.

Green Anole

The green anole is a lizard that lives in trees. It is also known as the Carolina anole and American anole. It is territorial and will fight other males to defend its area. To impress a female, the male dances and extends his colorful dewlap— the loose skin under his chin.

WHERE DO THEY LIVE?

They are found in the USA from southern Virginia to Florida and to eastern Texas.

USA ●

Sticky Feet

▶ Green anoles have sticky pads on their toes. These let them grip onto surfaces and allow them to climb walls.

DID YOU KNOW?

 If a predator grabs the anole's tail, the anole will cut its own tail off to escape and grow another tail.

It quenches its thirst by lapping up raindrops on leaves.

If a green anole accidentally falls out of a tree, it goes into a flat "skydiving" position to slow its fall.

Laying Eggs

▶ The female lays about 10 eggs each season. She buries these in soft soil. There the sun warms the earth and incubates the eggs, which will hatch in 30–45 days. The hatchlings must defend themselves— their parents do not look after them. Hatchlings can be eaten by larger reptiles and mammals, but may also be eaten by adult anoles.

Color Changes

◀ Its color ranges from the brightest greens to the darkest browns. If it is stressed, it will turn a shade of brown and a black semicircle will show behind the eyes.

FACTS

SIZE

• They grow 5–8 in (13–20 cm) long.

• They live for between five and 10 years.

• They can react aggressively to their own reflection.

Green Mamba

This swift, slim African snake spends most of its time high up in the trees. It is often found on plantations that grow mangoes, coconuts, and cashew nuts. It doesn't eat these, but it does eat the rats and birds that are attracted to the fruit.

Head

▶ Behind the eyes are the venom glands. It has solid teeth in both jaws and two large venom fangs.

WHERE DO THEY LIVE?

There are two species of green mamba. One lives in West Africa; the other lives in East Africa.

Africa

Shedding Skin

◀ They need to shed their skin to grow, but do not have rocks to rub against. Instead, they snag their skin on twigs and slide out of their old skin.

FACTS

SIZE

● It grows up to 8 ft (2.5 m).

● It can live between 15 and 25 years in the wild.

● As a snake that hunts by day, it has round pupils in its eyes.

DID YOU KNOW?

🖐 It has enlarged belly scales that give the snake a good grip as it climbs tall tree trunks.

🖐 Males compete for the attention of females by dancing with each other. Each male raises its head, threatening but not biting the other males in the dance.

🖐 Untreated green mamba bites can kill humans.

A Shy Snake

▶ Unlike its larger cousin the black mamba, the green mamba is shy. It would rather avoid contact with humans. It can move quickly—7 mph (11.3 km/h). If cornered, it might strike with its venomous fangs. It only hunts on the ground if prey cannot be found in trees.

Green Tree Python

The green tree python hangs from branches high in the forest canopy. Its green scales give it excellent camouflage. It waits very still for a long time for prey to pass. Then a bat, frog, or lizard comes too close and the python darts its head forward and bites.

WHERE DO THEY LIVE?

They live in the dense rain forests of New Guinea and on the northern tip of Australia.

New Guinea

Australia

Color

▶ Despite their name, young green tree pythons are usually yellow, but sometimes are orange or brick red. Some adults are yellow.

Body

◀ They have muscular bodies and can stretch themselves out straight to reach across to the next tree. They have large scales on their stomachs to help grip.

FACTS

SIZE

● They usually grow 3–4 ft (1–1.3 m).

● The female lays her 8–25 eggs on the ground in a tree stump.

● They live from sea level to an elevation of 5,905 ft (1,800 m).

DID YOU KNOW?

 The young green tree python wriggles its tail to make it look like a worm. This way it tricks prey into approaching it.

The female only needs to leave the trees to lay her eggs. Males may never leave the trees.

It takes 5–10 days for the young to change their color.

Head and Heat Sensors

▶ The black pupils at the center of the eyes narrow in the brightness of day. After dark they open out when the python sets off to hunt. The scales around the mouth can sense heat. The python can use these sensors to find prey or be aware of predators. It changes into its adult coloration after one to two years. Like all pythons, it is not venomous.

Indian Python

The Indian python is one of the biggest and strongest snakes in the world. It is a very powerful constrictor. It squeezes the life out of its prey before gobbling it up. It dangles by day from the low branches of trees. It attacks mammals, some birds, and reptiles.

Patterns

▶ Its markings camouflage it from young eagles and other predators, as well as from prey.

WHERE DO THEY LIVE?

They are found across Asia from Pakistan to southern China and as far south as Thailand and Vietnam.

Asia

Feeding

◀ Each year it only needs to eat its own weight in food to survive. It may eat most of this in one go and then spend months without eating at all.

FACTS

- They grow up to 21 ft (6.5 m).

- They can live up to 40 years.

- These snakes can survive underwater for many minutes.

SIZE

DID YOU KNOW?

The female guards her eggs and keeps them warm.

While looking after her eggs for between two and three months, the female won't feed and so can lose up to half her body weight.

The python can stretch itself out straight to reach another branch.

Hunting

▶ The vertical eye slits are narrow during the bright day, but they open wider at sunset when the python sets out to hunt. The muscular body can constrict large prey, but the rib cage can also open wide to make room for the prey in its stomach. An Indian python was once found with a grown leopard in its stomach.

King Cobra

The heavy and muscular king cobra is the largest venomous snake in the world. It can kill other snakes with its powerful venom, and uses its menacing hood to warn off other animals. Just one bite from this highly poisonous snake is enough to bring down an elephant. The king cobra can grow to 18 ft (5.5 m) long.

WHERE DO THEY LIVE?

Widespread, but mainly in the rain forests and plains of India, southern China, and southeast Asia.

Asia

DID YOU KNOW?

It is the only snake in the world that builds a nest for its eggs.

The king cobra is safe from the venom of its own kind. If one bites another, the venom has no effect.

After one large meal, the king cobra can go for weeks without needing to eat again.

Hood

▶ The cobra spreads its neck ribs to form the hood, which has false eyespots on it that may confuse or scare off predators.

Threat Display

▶ It rears its head off the ground and spreads its neck into a "hood" to present a terrifying threat display toward intruders and predators. It preys on other snakes, even other venomous species. It overcomes them with its venom and then swallows them. The king cobra is a shy snake and will avoid people, but it can be very aggressive if it is cornered and feels threatened.

Skin Color

◀ The skin is olive green, tan, or black, with faint, pale yellow cross-bands down the entire length of the body. The underbelly is cream or pale yellow.

FACTS

SIZE

● A single bite contains enough venom to kill 20 people.

● The fangs can grow to 0.5 in (1.25 cm) long.

● Snake charmers in south Asia use king cobras in their acts.

Komodo Dragon

The Komodo dragon is the heaviest and strongest lizard in the world. With a mouthful of sharklike teeth, powerful claws, and muscle-packed limbs, it can overpower animals much larger than itself. It eats by tearing off large chunks of flesh and swallowing them whole.

Waterproof

▶ It is covered in a waterproof, scaly skin. This stops the dragon drying out in the hot, tropical sunshine.

WHERE DO THEY LIVE?

Komodo, Rinca, Gili Motang, and Flores, part of the Lesser Sunda Islands in Indonesia.

Asia

Indonesia

Tongue

◀ The forked tongue is 12 in (30 cm) long. It flicks out to "taste" the air for traces of prey animals. When resting, the tongue is drawn back into the head.

FACTS

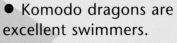
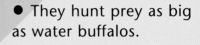

SIZE

• Komodo dragons are excellent swimmers.

• They hunt prey as big as water buffalos.

• They can live for 30 years or more.

DID YOU KNOW?

 The claws are long and very sharp. They can inflict fatal wounds. They also allow it to climb rocks and trees.

It has an elastic stomach that can expand to hold a huge amount of food, allowing the dragon to cram its belly full.

A dragon's bite may contain at least four poisonous bacteria.

Teeth

▶ The teeth of the Komodo dragon curve backward, helping the lizard grip struggling prey. The rear edges of the teeth are saw-edged like steak knives. New teeth replace old ones every three months, so the dragon always has a sharp set of butchering tools in its mouth.

Leaf-tailed Gecko

The leaf-tailed gecko is one of Madagascar's most unusual creatures. It has bulbous eyes, a gripping tail, and sticky toes, and is totally adapted to life in the rain forest. It has excellent camouflage skills, making it blend into its natural environment.

Toe Pads

▶ Each toe is covered with millions of bristles that end in tiny pads. These pads give the gecko a good grip on surfaces.

DID YOU KNOW?

🐾 The body is flat so it can easily slip into crevices during the day.

🐾 The flat tail is muscular and moves easily. It is covered with gripping pads, like the toes. The gecko uses its tail like an extra foot to grip tree bark.

🐾 It has more teeth than any other lizard.

WHERE DO THEY LIVE?

In mainland Madagascar and surrounding islands.

Madagascar

Camouflage

▶ The gecko can change its skin color to match its surroundings. This color change is most dramatic at night. Some gecko species are stunning, with bright colors from pinks to oranges. Others are a duller brown color. The camouflage on some of the leaf-tailed gecko species is so convincing that they can look like dead leaves on branches.

Long Tongue

◀ The tongue is long and sticky to catch insects. It does not have movable eyelids, so it cannot blink to clean its eyes. Instead it polishes its eyes with its long tongue.

FACTS

SIZE

- It can grow up to 8 in (20 cm) long.
- It eats insects, spiders, and other small invertebrates.
- Males make chirpy noises and click to attract females.

Marine Iguana

This unique black lizard spends much of its life shuffling between the baking rocks and the cold blue water. It is the only lizard that is fully adapted to marine life. It can stay underwater for long periods of time. It is also one of the few lizards that has a vegetarian diet.

WHERE DO THEY LIVE?

On rocky coasts of the Galapagos Islands in the eastern Pacific.

Galapagos Islands

South America

Scaly Skin

▶ The scaly skin is tough and waterproof to prevent injury and to keep it from drying out in the scorching sun.

Feet and Toes

◀ The feet have strong toes and unusually long claws. This lets the marine iguana cling to rocks and so resist being swept away by the often powerful waves.

FACTS

SIZE

● It might look fierce, but it is actually a gentle herbivore.

● All female iguanas are smaller than males.

● As the marine iguana grows, its skin continually peels away.

DID YOU KNOW?

At night, marine iguanas huddle together in groups to keep warm.

The tail is flattened sideways. It is used like an oar to drive the iguana through the water.

It stops itself from overheating by sitting in shady areas or plunging into the cold sea.

Crest and Nostril

▶ The marine iguana has a sawlike crest of horny spines along its back and tail, with longer spines on the nape of its neck. It has a special gland that opens into each nostril so the iguana can release unwanted salt from its system in a spray of salty water. The salt will often land on its head, giving it a distinctive white wig.

Massasauga

The massasauga is often known as a shy and sluggish snake. It doesn't like confrontation with humans, and when under threat it prefers to leave the area rather than strike out. Like any animal, though, it will protect itself if necessary. It has short fangs that can easily puncture skin, and these fangs have a powerful venom.

Massasauga

▶ "Massasauga" means "Great River Mouth" in the Chippewa language. It got this name by being found near rivers and lakes.

DID YOU KNOW?

It eats mainly small mammals (shrews and mice) and small snakes.

A bite from a massasauga can be very painful and life-threatening. But people are rarely bitten by them because of their shy behavior.

There are three subspecies of massasauga: the eastern, western, and desert populations.

WHERE DO THEY LIVE?

The United States from the Great Lakes down to the Mexican border.

USA ●

Rattle

◀ The rattle is smaller than that of a typical rattlesnake. When shaken, it warns enemies to keep well away. The rattle gets bigger every time the snake sheds its skin.

FACTS

SIZE

• Adults are 18–30 in (46–76 cm) long.

• Females give birth to between eight and 20 young in late summer.

• They are sometimes caught and sold illegally as pets.

Color and Markings

▶ The massasauga is usually gray, grayish-brown, or brown. The back has large, dark brown blotches with smaller, lighter brown patches on its sides. The young massasauga has similar markings, but it is more brightly colored. This snake is also known as the black rattler, sauger, black massasauga, swamp rattler, or gray rattlesnake.

Nile Crocodile

With its massive and powerful jaws, the Nile crocodile is a deadly threat to other creatures as it lurks beneath the water, waiting to snap them up. It is the largest reptile in Africa. It can grow up to 20 ft (6 m) from snout to tail and weighs more than 1,984 lb (900 kg).

WHERE DO THEY LIVE?

In Africa, south of the Sahara, along the River Nile, and in Madagascar.

Africa

Madagascar

Teeth

▶ Its teeth grow continuously. After about two years, the worn-out teeth are forced out by the sharp new ones underneath.

Fast Legs

◀ It walks with its legs splayed, but don't let the squashed look fool you: this animal can be fast. It has powerful feet and claws to climb up riverbanks.

FACTS

● It can eat up to half its body weight in a single feeding.

● Up to 90 percent of Nile crocodiles die in their first year.

● It guards its nest until the eggs hatch.

SIZE

DID YOU KNOW?

 The Nile crocodile can stay underwater for more than an hour as it waits to ambush prey.

It is so powerful that it can drag a fully grown zebra underwater in just a few seconds.

All crocodiles have an acidic stomach so they can digest bones, horns, and hooves.

Eyes and Nostrils

▶ The eyes sit above the head so that the crocodile can keep a lookout for prey while the rest of its body is under the water. The nostrils sit on a raised part of the snout. This allows the crocodile to breathe when the rest of its body is underwater. Flaps seal the nostrils to keep out water during dives. Clear "third eyelids" flick over to protect the eyes underwater.

Nile Monitor

Africa's largest lizard, the Nile monitor may be smaller than a Nile crocodile, but it can still try to steal a Nile crocodile's eggs. Like all monitors, it has a forked tongue and a strong sense of smell. It lays up to 40 eggs. As each egg weighs about 1.75 oz (50 g), pregnancy can double its weight.

DID YOU KNOW?

🐾 They are closely related to aigialosaurs, a group of monitors adapted to living in water that lived in the Cretaceous Period more than 65 million years ago.

🐾 Nile monitors are excellent swimmers.

🐾 They can remain underwater for up to an hour.

WHERE DO THEY LIVE?

Africa

They are found near watery spots in much of Africa except for the very dry areas in the north.

Nostrils

▶ Its nostrils are at the tip of its snout. It lives in the water with just its nose poking out, breathing in air.

Eating

▶ When Nile monitors are young, their teeth are sharp. When they become adults, their teeth become blunt. Their bodies are muscular. Their sharp claws are used for climbing, digging, defending themselves, and tearing at their prey. When scavenging at a carcass, they often try to swallow lumps that are far too big for them. They eat fish, snails, frogs, crocodile eggs, young snakes, birds, small mammals, large insects such as crickets, and dead animals they find.

Laying Eggs

◀ A female monitor sometimes breaks into a termite mound and lays her eggs. The termites quickly repair the hole, sealing the eggs in the safety of their nest.

FACTS

- They can grow up to 9 ft (2.7 m) long.
- Large adults weigh 22–26.5 lb (10–12 kg).
- They can live up to 15 years in captivity.

SIZE

Puff Adder

The puff adder is one of the most dangerous snakes in the whole of Africa. It kills many people every year. It lies in wait, hidden by its camouflage. When an unsuspecting victim walks by, it strikes with a quick and venomous bite. As it opens its mouth, its fangs swing down on hinges. The adder thrusts its fangs deep into its prey.

Camouflage

▶ The coloring and skin pattern of the puff adder help it to blend into its natural surroundings.

WHERE DO THEY LIVE?

Throughout Africa and parts of the Arabian Peninsula.

Saudi Arabia

Africa

Short Body

◀ The body of the puff adder is short and thick. Rippling the big scales on its belly, the snake creeps forward in a straight line, like a giant caterpillar.

FACTS

SIZE

● Every 10 weeks or so one fang falls out and a new one replaces it.

● Puff adders can swim and climb trees.

● One puff adder may have enough venom to kill 4–5 people.

DID YOU KNOW?

It coils up into a tight "S" shape just before it strikes its prey.

A young puff adder can hunt and kill small prey almost straight after being born.

It takes its name from the way it puffs up its thick-set body to frighten both predators and prey.

Venom and Attack

▶ The extra-large venom glands lie at the back of the jaw. They make the snake's flattened head much wider than its neck. The long fangs fold back like a switchblade when the snake closes its mouth. When threatened or ready to attack, the puff adder sucks air in through its nostrils to inflate its body.

Rattlesnake

There are 32 species of rattlesnake, and all of them are native to the Americas. They are predators and kill their prey with a venomous bite. The venom destroys body tissue and causes internal bleeding. Some rattlesnakes have a toxin that can paralyze. The rattle of the tail warns predators off, but hawks, weasels, and king snakes can kill rattlesnakes.

Hearing

▶ They do not have ears on the outside of their bodies. Their hearing is weak, but they can feel vibrations in the ground.

WHERE DO THEY LIVE?

They are found in the Americas, from southern Canada to central Argentina.

North America

Central America

South America

Tongue

◄ They can smell with their nostrils and also with their tongues. The tongue carries the scent to an organ in the roof of the mouth, which identifies it.

FACTS

SIZE

• They grow up to 6 ft 6 in (2.1 m) long.

• They weigh up to 12 lb (5 kg).

• In captivity, they can live for up to 30 years.

DID YOU KNOW?

✋ The rings that make up the rattle are actually dried skin from when the snake has molted.

✋ The rattlesnake travels with its rattle held up to try to protect it from damage.

✋ Its bite can be fatal to humans if not treated quickly, but a rattlesnake only bites if provoked.

Looking for Prey

► Two pits, one in front of each eye, can sense heat over a short range of 1 ft (0.3 m). The rattlesnake uses these to find and aim at prey. Each eye has a vertical slit pupil that opens wide in the dark to let in as much light as possible. It can see some colors but cannot see shapes very well. It relies on seeing movement.

Reticulated Python

The reticulated python is the world's longest snake. It can grow to the length of a school bus. Not only that, it can eat animals as large as pigs and deer. "Reticulated" means "like a net" because of the crisscross pattern on the snake's back. It is not venomous, but kills by squeezing.

Camouflage

▶ In the shadows of the jungle, their brown-yellow patterned skin is well-camouflaged among fallen leaves.

WHERE DO THEY LIVE?

Asia

They are found in rain forests, woodlands, grasslands, and rivers across southeast Asia.

Head

◀ It has bright orange eyes with vertical pupils. It has 100 teeth and two sharp fangs. A special tube in its mouth lets it breathe when its mouth is full of food.

FACTS

SIZE

- On average it grows to 10–20 ft (3–6 m).

- A baby hatchling will already be 2 ft (60 cm) long.

- It can live for up to 20 years.

DID YOU KNOW?

The reticulated python is an excellent swimmer. It has swum offshore to settle on islands.

Its body is slimmer than other constrictors. It can weigh half what an anaconda of the same length weighs.

It can be a danger to humans, but attacks are very rare.

Feeding

▶ It mainly hunts by lying in wait and ambushing. As a constrictor snake, it wraps its body around its prey and squeezes until its prey stops breathing. Then it swallows the prey whole. Near human populations, it can snatch chickens, cats, and dogs. It can loosen its jaws to swallow prey up to one-quarter its own length and the same as its own weight.

Rhinoceros Viper

The rhinoceros viper gets its name from the two or three sets of scales like horns on the end of its nose. It is known for its bright blue or blue-green oblong markings, each with a yellow line down the center. It hunts by ambush, killing small mammals, toads, frogs, and fish.

Camouflage

▶ The color pattern allows it to blend in among the leaves in the mix of sun and shade on the forest floor.

DID YOU KNOW?

🖐 It uses its rough scales to grip when it is moving. It slithers by stretching and then releasing its skin.

🖐 It mainly lives on the ground but can also climb trees.

🖐 The sensor on the top of the mouth of all snakes that identifies scents passed to it by the tongue is called the Jacobson's organ.

WHERE DO THEY LIVE?

They live in tropical rain forests in Central and West Africa.

Africa

Fangs and Attack

▶ After a strike, the rhinoceros viper immediately pulls back. It does this to avoid breaking its fangs in a struggle. Also, it doesn't always bite with its pair of fangs (it can use its other teeth). And it doesn't always release venom. But just in case, it has up to six replacement pairs of fangs growing in different stages of development.

Head

◀ The rhinoceros viper can attack in any direction. It can throw its head forward, backward, or sideways with startling speed.

FACTS

- It grows up to 6 ft (1.8 m) long.

- It can live for up to 15 years.

- It is mainly active at night.

SIZE

Rinkhals

The rinkhals does not have to bite—it can simply spit venom in its enemy's face. It can spray its venom 8 ft (2.5 m). To do this, it has to rear up its head and throw its body forward to release the venom. However, it sometimes avoids a fight by rolling onto its back, opening its mouth, and pretending to be dead. If it feels threatened, it spreads its hood, showing its striped neck.

WHERE DO THEY LIVE?

They are found in swamps and as high as mountain slopes in southern and southeastern Africa.

Africa

Scales

▶ Unlike true cobras, rinkhals' scales are not flat but have ridges. Some rinkhals have black bodies; others are striped.

Offspring

◀ Most snakes lay eggs, but rinkhals' eggs hatch inside the mother. She usually gives birth to between 20 and 30 live young. The young are already venomous when born.

FACTS

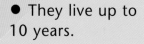

SIZE

● On average they grow to 3 ft (1 m) long.

● They live up to 10 years.

● They are the only snakes with front fangs that give birth to live young.

DID YOU KNOW?

✋ If disturbed, it prefers to try to scare others away rather than use its precious venom.

✋ It gets its name from the bands on its throat. "Rinkhals" means "ring neck" in the Afrikaans language.

✋ Its venom can be deadly to humans but the rinkhals doesn't generally attack people.

Spitting

▶ Spitting snakes probably developed their unusual means of defense in the way that rattlesnakes developed rattles. Painful sprays and noisy rattles are both good ways of stopping big animals such as buffalos trampling you to death. By not biting, they are not risking losing their fangs.

Savannah Monitor

The main predators for the savannah monitor are snakes, birds, and people. It protects itself through camouflage. If threatened, it usually runs away or plays dead. But if cornered, it can defend itself by flicking its tail like a whip and by biting.

Diet

▶ When young it feeds on millipedes and crickets. In adulthood it eats scorpions and frogs.

WHERE DO THEY LIVE?

Africa

They live in West and Central Africa from Senegal to western Ethiopia.

Attack

◀ When attacked, it can roll onto its back and hold its hind leg in its mouth, forming a ring. This makes it harder for a predator to swallow the monitor.

FACTS

SIZE

- Adults are 3–5 ft (1–1.5 m) long.
- They weigh 4–10 lb (2–4 kg).
- They can live up to 30 years.

DID YOU KNOW?

🖐 In the wet season, its tail grows full of fat. It can live off this fat in the dry months.

🖐 Millipedes release a foul-tasting fluid to defend against monitors. But the monitor rubs them first with its chin, so that they release all their fluid. Only then does it snap them up.

Thick Skin

▶ Its skin is very thick, so it keeps moisture inside and is not burnt by the sun. This allows it to live in dry areas many miles from the nearest river or waterhole. However, it cannot survive for long in the real desert. Although it lives in such dry areas, it is a surprisingly good swimmer. Its skin is often sold for leather to make shoes, handbags, and watch straps.

Shingleback Skink

The shingleback skink is a short-tailed and slow-moving lizard, but it has a special defensive trick. Its tail looks a little bit like its head and this may be used to confuse predators. The tail also contains fat reserves, which it can draw upon when it is hibernating in winter.

WHERE DO THEY LIVE?

Australia

It is found across southern Australia in dry habitats across to western Australia.

Blue Tongue

▶ Its blue tongue is designed to surprise. One glimpse of it makes some predators run away.

Offspring

◄ Males fight in the spring for the attention of females. Most blue-tongued skinks give birth to 25 live young, but the shingleback only gives birth to up to four.

FACTS

SIZE

- They grow up to 16 in (40 cm) long.
- They weigh up to 2 lb (1 kg).
- They can live up to 40 years.

DID YOU KNOW?

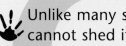

🖐 Unlike many skinks, it cannot shed its tail.

🖐 Because of the shape of its tail, it is sometimes known as the "two-headed skink."

🖐 The young stay with their parents for many months. Then they join a colony of closely related skinks.

Food Chain

▶ It is an omnivore, eating both animal and plant matter. It feeds on snails, dead insects, leaves, flowers, and fruits. It is preyed upon by dingos (Australian wild dogs), Australian pythons, foxes, and wildcats. Its bite is not venomous, but the bacteria from its mouth may infect wounds.

Thorny Devil

Living in the desert, the thorny devil needs to make use of what little water there is. The ridges and sharp spikes on its body not only make it look fierce and defend it but stop water rolling off. When dew settles on its body, grooves in the skin draw it to the thorny devil's mouth. If its feet are in water, the water will move up the skin grooves to the mouth.

False Head

▶ It has a spiny "false head" on the back of its neck. It presents this to predators by dipping its real head.

WHERE DO THEY LIVE?

It lives in the dry and hot inland parts of western and central Australia.

Australia

DID YOU KNOW?

Predators of the thorny devil include wild birds, blue-tongued lizards, and monitor lizards.

It is the only species of the genus *Moloch* and so it is sometimes known as a moloch.

The largest females are twice as heavy as males.

Camouflage

◀ Its coloring allows it to blend in with the dry scrubland floor, where it looks like twigs and dry leaves. Its colors are brighter in summer and darker in winter.

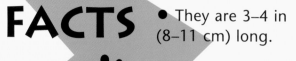

FACTS

SIZE

- They are 3–4 in (8–11 cm) long.

- They weigh 1–3 oz (35–90 g).

- They live up to 20 years.

Feeding

▶ The thorny devil will eat thousands of ants a day. But small twigs, tiny flowers, and insect eggs have also been found in its stomach. The ants it ate were probably carrying these when they were eaten. During rainfalls it can drink by sucking in water from all over its body.

Tiger Snake

It is called a tiger snake because of the 40 to 50 yellow or cream cross-bands along its back. These contrast with the background color, which may be brown, olive, or green. Its body is thicker and stouter than that of many snakes. It flattens its body when lying in the sun to absorb more warmth. It also flattens its body when threatened.

WHERE DO THEY LIVE?

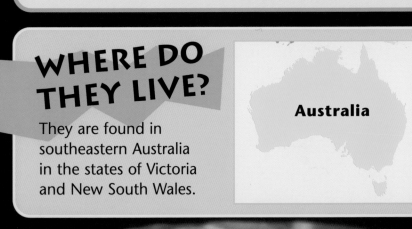

Australia

They are found in southeastern Australia in the states of Victoria and New South Wales.

DID YOU KNOW?

The tiger snake can hunt underwater for up to nine minutes.

The bite of the death adder, which is very dangerous to humans, has little effect on tiger snakes.

The tiger snake can climb trees to prey on nesting birds.

Parasites

▶ Living inside or on the bodies of tiger snakes can be ticks, tapeworms, roundworms, and tongue worms.

Diet and Hunting

▶ The tiger snake mainly eats frogs, but living in southeast Australia where there are the most people, buildings, and cities it is now harder to find enough frogs. So, the tiger snake also eats lizards, birds, small mammals, and fish. It mainly hunts by day but during the warmer months will hunt at night. It catches its prey and then uses venom to weaken it.

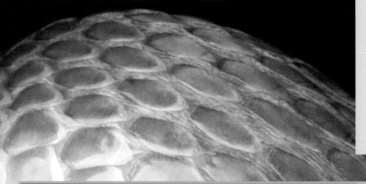

Offspring

◀ The tiger snake produces living young (usually 20–30) rather than laying eggs. This is an adaptation to living in a temperate rather than a tropical climate.

FACTS

SIZE

• They usually grow to 3 ft (1 m) long.

• They can live for more than 17 years in captivity.

• Their fangs are 0.25 in (3.5 mm) long.

American Alligator

In cooler regions, the American alligator becomes inactive during winter months. It digs a cozy den under banks and stays there for up to four months, moving little and seldom eating. Sometimes it even becomes frozen in, but as long as there's a breathing hole, it can survive.

WHERE DO THEY LIVE?

They are found in wetlands in the southeastern USA.

USA ●

Lookout

▶ With its eyes on the same level as its mouth, it can keep a lookout while hiding most of its body underwater.

Water

◀ Its tail makes up half the body's length. The tail propels it through water. Although generally slow-moving on land, it can swim very quickly.

FACTS

- Males are larger than females and can grow up to 12 ft (3.6 m).

- They weigh up to 496 lb (225 kg).

- They live up to 50 years in captivity.

SIZE

DID YOU KNOW?

 They eat fish, birds, turtles, snakes, insects, snails, spiders, and worms. Adults will also eat raccoons and deer.

 They have the strongest laboratory-measured bite of any animal.

They are freshwater animals but will swim into brackish (mixed saltwater and freshwater) areas.

Roar!

▶ The male American alligator's roar carries for 492 ft (150 m). He often mistakes the loud noises of car horns, jet engines, jackhammers, and drills for the calls of rivals. He responds to these noises by hissing or bellowing. Female alligators are very protective and will guard their young for many years, mainly from other alligators.

Gharial

One of the longest-living of all crocodiles, the gharial can live up to 100 years. Although it grows up to 23 ft (7 m) long, it begins life very small: the hatchlings are roughly 15 in (37 cm) long. Males have a growth on the end of the snout. This is connected to its nostrils, through which it hisses. The growth amplifies the hisses, which are used to communicate.

Water Lover

▶ A gharial spends more time in the water than other crocodilians. It only leaves the water to bask in the sun or to nest.

WHERE DO THEY LIVE?

They are found in the rivers of northern India, Pakistan, Bangladesh, Nepal, and Bhutan.

India

Teeth

◀ Armed with more than 100 sharp teeth, the gharial loves to eat catfish. Its teeth are regularly replaced throughout its long life.

FACTS

SIZE

● Young gharials eat insects and small frogs.

● The female buries eggs in a hole on land. The hatchlings dig themselves out.

● The gharial is on the critically endangered list.

DID YOU KNOW?

🖐 Its name refers to the growth on its snout— "ghara" means "pot" in some Indian languages.

🖐 It is not a man-eater and cannot eat large animals, such as humans.

🖐 It once lived in all the major rivers in the Indian subcontinent, but now its range is much smaller.

Moving

▶ The gharial's leg muscles are not strong enough to lift it off the ground, so it cannot walk on land. But it can slide along on its belly and push itself forward with its legs. In the water though, it is the fastest crocodile in the world. It can reach 25 mph (40 km/h) when chasing fish, its long tail and webbed rear feet helping it move quickly.

Alligator Snapping Turtle

The alligator snapping turtle is the largest freshwater turtle in North America. It has a large, heavy head with a thick shell with ridges. These make it look a little like a plated dinosaur.

Underwater

▶ The alligator snapping turtle can stay underwater for up to 50 minutes before it must swim to the surface for air.

DID YOU KNOW?

🖐 Hunted by humans for food, it is now an endangered animal.

🖐 The male never leaves the water if it doesn't have to. The female only goes on dry land to lay eggs.

🖐 Warmer eggs become female, while cooler eggs become male.

WHERE DO THEY LIVE?

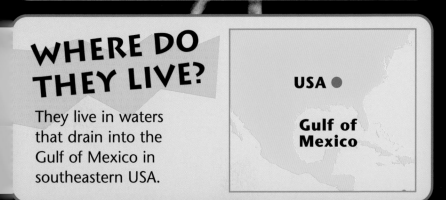

USA ●

Gulf of Mexico

They live in waters that drain into the Gulf of Mexico in southeastern USA.

Jaws

◀ It can open its enormous jaws to catch prey. The grip between its jaws is very strong—even after its head has been cut from its body it holds on.

FACTS

SIZE

- The body is 30 in (80 cm) long, plus a tail of the same length.

- It weighs up to 176 lb (80 kg).

- It can live up to 70 years in captivity.

Snapping Turtle Head

▶ Its eyes are surrounded by a star-shaped arrangement of pieces of flesh. These look a little like eyelashes. The patterns around the eyes help break up the shape of the eye and so keep it camouflaged. During the day it lurks in weeds and dangles a wormlike part of its tongue to lure fish, mollusks, frogs, reptiles, and mammals.

Mata Mata

The mata mata kills most of its prey by sucking them into its mouth. It spends much of its time very still on the beds of streams. Algae grow on its rough, ridged back, which can help to camouflage its shape. Although many turtles can draw their heads back into their shells, the mata mata is among those that cannot.

Suction

▶ It sucks in water, pulling its prey into its mouth. Then it pushes the water out and swallows the prey whole.

DID YOU KNOW?

🖐 It is carnivorous, eating only fish and aquatic invertebrates.

🖐 Its jaws don't have any teeth: they are made for swallowing animals whole, not chewing.

🖐 It grows fleshy, hanging parts on its throat. These may help camouflage it, making it look more like a water plant.

WHERE DO THEY LIVE?

They live in northern South America, especially the Orinoco and Amazon river basins.

South America

Neck

◀ Its neck is almost as long as its shell. It is known as a side-necked turtle because it protects its head by turning it sideways under the overhang at the front of the shell.

FACTS

SIZE

- Its shell is up to 18 in (45 cm) long.

- It weighs 5–6 lb (2.5 kg).

- It can live for up to 30 years in captivity.

Breathing

▶ The nose of the mata mata acts like a snorkel, sucking in air from the water's surface. Although it is an aquatic species (it only lives in water), it stands in shallow water, where its snout can reach the surface to breathe. Some turtles can take in a small amount of oxygen through the skin, but all also have to breathe at the surface of the water.

Snapping Turtle

We know that turtles can defend themselves by retreating inside their shells, but the snapping turtle can't completely do this: it is too large to hide inside its own shell. Perhaps because it can't defend itself as well, it has developed its aggressive snapping character.

WHERE DO THEY LIVE?

They are found in North, Central, and South America, from southern Canada down to Ecuador.

North America

Central America

South America

DID YOU KNOW?

- They live in shallow ponds, shallow lakes, and streams.

- Although they usually hibernate in mud in winter, they have been seen walking on frozen waters and swimming under the ice.

- In water, they usually avoid humans, but on land they might bite.

Smell

▶ When disturbed the snapping turtle often releases a powerful, musky scent. The older the turtle, the stronger the smell.

Appearance

▶ The beak is a sharp hook made of the same material as horn. The nostrils are at the very tip of the snout. The turtle can lie in the water with all its body under the surface except for its nostrils, which breathe in air. An omnivore, it eats both plant and animal matter. It is a scavenger, eating what it can find, but also a hunter, eating fish, frogs, snakes, smaller turtles, birds, small mammals, and invertebrates.

Body

◀ Its feet are webbed to help it swim. Its neck is very flexible. The top shell—called a carapace—is thick, hard, and a muddy color. This provides camouflage in the bottom of rivers.

FACTS

- They can grow to over 3 ft (1 m).
- They weigh up to 35 lb (16 kg).
- They can live for more than 45 years.

SIZE

Stinkpot Turtle

Stinkpots spend almost all their time in slow-moving creeks. They leave the water in two cases: the female lays her eggs on land, and adult turtles climb up to 6 ft (2 m) up riverside tree branches to bask in the sun. Then they drop back from the branches into the water.

Smell

▶ It gets its name from its ability to release a foul musky odor from the glands on the edge of its shell.

WHERE DO THEY LIVE?

They are found in shallow, muddy rivers in eastern North America.

North America

Diet

◀ They are carnivorous, eating worms, snails, crayfish, freshwater clams and mussels, insects, frogs, fish, and dead animals that they find.

FACTS

● They are 3–6 in (8–15 cm) long.

● They weigh around 1 lb 5 oz (600 g).

● They can be recognized by the yellow lines on their necks.

SIZE

DID YOU KNOW?

🖐 They hibernate in the mud for five or six months under logs or in muskrat lodges.

🖐 They have been known to fall from riverside tree branches into boats passing below.

🖐 Their tiny tongues are covered in buds that allow them to breathe underwater.

Reproduction

▶ The female lays up to nine eggs in a shallow burrow or under pieces of broken wood along the shoreline. Females share nesting sites, with up to 16 nests under one log. Eggs hatch in late summer or early fall. Hatchlings are usually less than 1 in (2.5 cm) long. They live for more than 50 years.

Glossary

Algae – sea plants

Ambush – lying in wait to attack by surprise

Amphibian – a class of animals that includes frogs, newts, and salamanders

Amplify – to make more intense, stronger, or louder

Arid – dry

Bacteria – tiny, single-cell organisms that often play a part in the decay of living things

Brille – a layer of see-through skin or scale covering the eyes of snakes and other reptiles

Camouflage – a method of hiding by disguising the body using colors and patterns

Carcass – the body of a dead animal

Carnivore – a meat-eater

Continent – one of the Earth's seven major areas of land. The continents are Africa, Antarctica, Asia, Australia, Europe, North America, and South America.

Dewlap – a loose fold of skin below the neck

Dislocate – to put out of proper place

Endangered – the risk of no more of the species being alive

Habitat – the environment where an animal naturally lives

Hatchling – a newborn animal from a hard-shelled egg, such as a young bird

Herbivore – a plant-eater

Hibernation – a time when some animals become less active in order to conserve energy. They slow down the speed at which they breathe, lower their body temperature, and survive on stored fat.

Incubate/incubation – to keep eggs warm until ready to hatch

Ligament – a band of tough tissue that connects bones or supports muscles or organs

Mammal – a warm-blooded animal with fur or hair on its skin and a skeleton inside its body. For example, humans, elephants, cows, and dogs.

Mollusk – the group of animals including squid, octopus, and snails. Most mollusks have a shell.

Omnivore – an animal that eats both animals and plant matter

Parasite – a smaller animal, such as a flea or a tapeworm, that feeds off a living larger one

Prehistoric – belonging to a period in time before written history

Reptile – a class of cold-blooded animals that includes lizards, snakes, and turtles

Savannah – a flat grassland in tropical or subtropical regions

Scavenger – an animal that eats the dead remains of other creatures

Scrubland – land on which the natural vegetation is low trees and shrubs

Semiaquatic – spending a large amount of time underwater

Subcontinent – a large, partly separate land mass that is part of a continent

Temperate climate – the climate zones between the polar regions and the tropics. These zones range between cool to warm. They include North America and Europe.

Territorial – living within a specific range

Toxic – poisonous

Tropical climate – a hotter climate found in the region between the Tropic of Cancer and the Tropic of Capricorn

Venom – like a poison, but venom is received through bites and stings

Index

Picture Credits

Big Stock: 89b Kevin Sibley; **Corbis**: 60/61 Ocean, 74/75 David Northcott; **Dreamstime**: 1, 44t Burtonhill, 11t Martin Krause, 13t Bernard Richter, 13b Vjrithwik, 17t Mikhail Blajenov, 17b, 18/19, 19b, 29b, 47b, 68/69, 73b, 77b, 79t, 82/83, 95t Mgkuijpers, 19t, 73t Robin Winkelman, 21b Wouter Van Der Wiel, 22/23 Eric Isselee, 25t, 67t Outdoorsman, 33t Brooke Whatnall, 33b Rosco, 35b Fotografescu, 36/37 Cosmin Manci, 37 both Lars Kastilian, 39b Gary Bridger, 43t Hudakore, 43b Rusty Dodson, 44b Sean Murray, 46/47 Saipg, 47t Aleksandr Bondarchiuk, 49t, 71b, 89t Lukas Blazek, 49b Rodolfo Clix, 51t Rokro, 55b Iorboaz, 56/57, 57l Cathy Keifer, 59t Brendan Van Son, 59b Matthew Ragen, 62t Steve Allen, 63b Martin Muller, 65l Melva, 65b AMWU, 67b Nico Smit, 69t Jason Mintzer, 71t Stef Bennett, 77t Anurax, 79b Sally Dexter, 81b Mark & Cressie, 83t Anthony Ngo, 85t Bonnie Fink, 87t Bornholm, 87b Martin Muransky, 9ll Dave Willman, 91r Kevin Adams; **FLPA**: 8/9 Ingo Schulz, 10/11, 20/21, 58/59, 84/85, 92/93 Pete Oxford, 12/13, 24/25, 25b, 26/27, 32/33, 66/67, 70/71, 78/79 Michael & Patricia Fogden, 14/15, 28/29, 72/73 Chris Mattison, 16/17, 44/45, 48/49 Gerry Ellis, 30/31 Bill Draker, 34/35 Mark Moffett, 38/39, 39t Chien Lee, 40/41 Gerard Lacz, 42/43 Albert Lleal, 50/51 Jany Sauvanet/Photo Researchers, 52/53 Manoal Ranjit, 54/55 Stephen Belcher, 62/63, 64/65 Frans Lanting, 75t Karl Sitak/Photo Researchers, 78/79 Neil Bowman, 80/81, 91t Cyril Ruoso, 86/87 Kevin Schafer, 88/89 James Robinson/Photo Researchers, 90/91 Ron Austing, 94/95 James Fisher/Photo Researchers; iStock: 91b Mark Kostich; **Christopher Murray**: 27b; **Ontley**: 95b Creative Commons Attribution-Share Alike 3.0 Unported License; **Photos.com**: 21t, 53l; **Photoshot**: 38/39, 75b ANT; **Public Domain**: 61b; **Shutterstock**: 6, 41t K Kaplin, 11b Collette3, 15t Sailorr, 15b JMiks, 23t Four Oaks, 23b Stu Porter, 27t Madov, 29t Wouter Tolenaars, 31t Spllogics, 31b James De Boer, 35t Horia Bogden, 41b, 53r, 57r, 85b Eric Isselee, 51b Mambo6435, 55t Beltsazar, 61t Gerald A De Boer, 69b N Frey Photography, 81t Urosr, 83t Eco Print; **US Fish & Wildlife Services**: 3, 9 both